Madsen

DRAWING ANIMALS!

A SHOW-HOW GUIDE!

Written & illustrated
by Keith Zoo

ODD DOT • NEW YORK

Hey there!

This **Show-How** gives you the know-how on drawing animals. We've included only the essentials so you can easily master the FUN-damentals. With a little practice, you'll soon be drawing a whole zoo! Ready? Let's go!

MATERIALS NEEDED:

PAPER
(ANYTHING WORKS—PRINTER PAPER,
CRAFT PAPER, SCRAP PAPER, ETC.)

DRAWING TOOLS
(PENCIL, ERASER, PEN, MARKER, CRAYON)

You can use anything to draw, but start out with a pencil first so you can erase your lines.

TABLE OF CONTENTS

ESSENTIAL DRAWING BASICS

1 *LINE & SHAPE* 4

2 *FORM & SHADING* 8

3 *TEXTURE & DETAIL* 12

4 *SPACE* 14

HOW TO DRAW ANIMALS

5 *PETS* 18

   DOG, CAT, HAMSTER, BIRD

6 *FARM ANIMALS* 24

   COW, PIG, LLAMA, HORSE

7 *FOREST CREATURES* 30

   FOX, BEAR, SQUIRREL, HEDGEHOG

8 *SAFARI ANIMALS* 36

   ELEPHANT, GIRAFFE

9 *REPTILES & AMPHIBIANS* 40

   SNAKE, FROG, LIZARD

10 *AQUATIC ANIMALS* 44

   FISH, WHALE

GETTING STARTED

Animals are super fun to draw. There are so many possibilities!
Before we begin, though, we need to cover a few drawing basics.
After that, we'll jump into creating some favorite animals, step-by-step.
By the end of this book, you'll be ready to draw your own critters!

1

LINE & SHAPE

The most basic element of drawing—and the building block of everything that follows—is the **point**. It is the simplest of marks. Take your drawing tool and make a tiny dot on your page. That's a point.

POINT

When drawing a **line**, first make a point. Then, hold down and drag your drawing tool in any direction.

STARTING POINT   *LINE*

Hooray! You've made a line.

In this book, you will use two line weights that look like this:

Sketch line—a light, rough line done in pencil (can be erased)

Final line—a darker, heavier, more defined line (as a last step)

TYPES OF LINES:

STRAIGHT *CURVED* *WAVY* *SQUIGGLE* *SCALLOPED* *ZIGZAG*

Now that we've covered lines, let's follow up with **shape**.
A shape is the two-dimensional design created when you connect lines together. Some basic shapes are a circle, square, triangle, and rectangle—but you can create any shape you like.

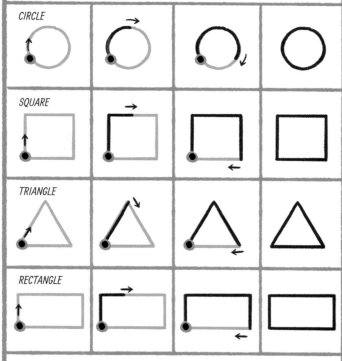

CIRCLE

SQUARE

TRIANGLE

RECTANGLE

Here are some more shapes you'll see in this book:

TEARDROP   CLOUD   OVAL   CRESCENT   HEART   FOOTBALL   DIAMOND

Shapes can be used as the building blocks for your design.
Let's combine some and make a character!

1

Imagine which shapes you want to start with

2

Sketch those shapes, overlapping them in interesting ways

3

Sketch in the basic body, then erase overlapping lines

4

Try adding some limbs and variety

5

Now add the character details, like eyes, nose, and a mouth

6

Add even more details—fur, a tail, etc.

TIP: Arrows point to lines that should be erased.

A cloud shape makes a great bunny tail!

7

2

FORM & SHADING

Form makes a two-dimensional shape look more three dimensional. Think to yourself, *What does this animal look like in the real world?*

For example, let's look at this circle. This flat shape has no depth!

Now imagine a ball you can hold in your hand. Think about what it would look like if you then wrapped a piece of string around it. You would see the string bend and curve around the back, then come around the front. Lines would bend around the form.

HIGHLIGHT

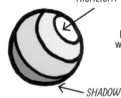

SHADOW

Adding **shading** helps create form by providing shadows and highlights. This will give the illusion of thickness, volume, and depth to make your drawing look more real.

Let's take a look at this shape. You can see the arrow starting underneath, going behind, then up and around to the front. Notice how going from light to dark gives the illusion that this shape is round, like it is being lit from above. This is called **gradation**!

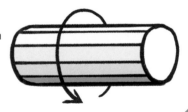

Shading can be done in several different ways. You can use a combination of lines and points to create a believable gradation on your form.

HATCHING
Going in one direction, draw a series of parallel lines. The farther apart they are, the lighter it will look. Closer together, the area will start looking darker.

CROSS HATCHING
Similar to hatching. After you make one set of lines, add a new set going in a different direction. Hence the name "cross hatch"!

POINTILLISM
Like hatching, but using only points—lots of them! The closer they are, the darker the area will look.

SOLID
Fill in all areas that would look as though they are in shadow, so there is no gradation. It is one solid, uniform shadow. In games and cartoons, this technique is called "cel-shading." This method works best with markers or watercolor.

When shading, the first step is to fill in your basic values: light, medium, and dark. This will help you see how the different areas are separated before you add volume to your form.

LIGHT   MEDIUM   DARK

As a final example, let's imagine our little bunny from Chapter 1. What would happen if we lit him from the top, the bottom, the left, and the right? Let's see that solid shading in action!

3
TEXTURE & DETAIL

Texture and detail can really bring your illustrations to life!
We collected some cool examples you can try out.

FEATHERS

LONG FUR & HAIR

SHORT FUR & HAIR

WOOD

STONE

LIQUID

ROCK

4
SPACE

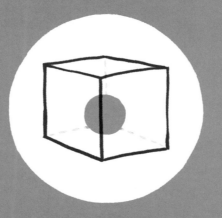

Imagine your drawing in **space**. Nope, not moons and stars.
We're talking about how your drawing exists in its own world with other
things around it. Think of the bunny drawing from Chapter 1.
How would you draw other things around it?

Say that this new space is a box, and we are creating a little scene with the
bunny in that box. Place the bunny right in the middle.
The box has a front, a middle, and a back.

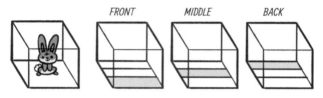

FRONT   *MIDDLE*   *BACK*

If you were to look through a camera,
you'd see something like this:

This is called the **picture plane**!
It's how you visualize space and
represent how it looks on paper
from the viewer's **point of view**.

The "front" of the box is what we would   The "middle" is the **midground**.
call the **foreground**. It's everything   It's the middle area, right where
that is sitting closest to the camera.   the bunny is placed.

The "back" is the
background. It's
everything that sits
behind both the
foreground and
midground, farthest
from the camera.

Now that we've placed our bunny in space, let's draw a few props:

FOREGROUND: *PINE TREE*

1

Sketch a few triangles and lines to create your pine tree

2

Erase overlapping lines and add some grass

3

Add texture and detail

MIDGROUND: *BUNNY DEN*

1

Sketch a few basic shapes to create the structure of your den

2

Add more basic shapes

3

Add texture and detail

BACKGROUND: *MOUNTAINS*

1

Sketch using squiggle lines to create your mountain shape

2

Add more lines (wavy, scalloped, etc.)

3

Add texture and detail

All right! Remember, using the templates on the left, draw your props in each of the sections within the scene.

Here is an example of what it could look like all together:

MIDGROUND

BACKGROUND

FOREGROUND

Add texture and detail.

Let's add shading to give some depth to the forms!

Now that you have the fundamentals, it's time to draw some animals!

5

PETS

DOG · CAT · HAMSTER · BIRD

DOG

1

Sketch some basic shapes to create the head and body of your dog

2

Erase overlapping lines, then sketch the tongue

3

Erase overlapping lines, then add a tail, eyes, and ears

4

Erase overlapping lines, then add legs

5

Add more details, like an eye patch, a collar, and a filled-in nose

6

Finalize your lines with a marker or pen

CAT

1

Sketch some basic shapes to create the head and body of your cat

2

Erase overlapping lines, then add ears, snout, and neck

3

Add eyes and collar

4

Add pupils, nose, and mouth

5

Erase overlapping lines, then add front and back legs

6

Add tail

7

Add details to ears and zigzag lines for furry cheeks

8

Add more details, like whiskers

9

Finalize your lines with a marker or pen

HAMSTER

1

Sketch some basic shapes to create the head and body of your hamster

2

Erase overlapping lines, then add eyes, nose, and mouth detail

3

Erase overlapping lines, then add arms, legs, and tail

4

Erase overlapping lines, then add hands

5

Add more details, like feet, inner ears, and fur

6

Finalize your lines with a marker or pen

BIRD

1

Sketch some basic shapes to create the head and body of your bird

2

Erase overlapping lines, then add feathers, wing, and tail

3

Add belly, eyes, and beak

4

Add feet

5

Add more details to the wings and tail

6

Finalize your lines with a marker or pen

DOG BONE

1

Draw two straight lines

2

Connect on one side with a scalloped line

3

Repeat on other side

CAT SCRATCHING POST

1

Draw two basic shapes

2

Connect them with two straight lines and erase overlapping lines

3

Add details and texture

HAMSTER CAGE

1

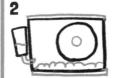

Draw a circle and rectangles

2

Add a few details

3

Add straight lines to make cage

BIRD CAGE

1

Sketch some basic shapes

2

Add horizontal and vertical lines and fill in base

3

Add more lines to make the cage bars

6

FARM ANIMALS

COW · PIG · LLAMA · HORSE

COW

1

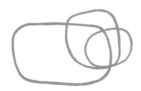

Sketch some basic shapes to create the head, body, and nose of your cow

2

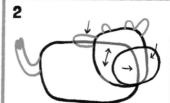

Erase overlapping lines, then add a tail, ears, and horns

3

Add ear details, eyes, nostrils, and mouth

4

Erase overlapping lines, then add legs and udder

5

Add spots and under-eye detail

6

Finalize your lines with a marker or pen

PIG

1

Sketch some basic shapes
to create the head, body, and
snout of your pig

2

Erase overlapping lines, then
add ears and connect the snout
to the head

3

Add a mouth, eyes, and nostrils

4

Erase overlapping lines,
then add feet

5

Add more details,
like hair and a tail

6

Finalize your lines
with a marker or pen

LLAMA

1

Sketch some basic shapes to create the head, body, and nose of your llama

2

Erase overlapping lines, then sketch a scalloped line to create fur and a tail

3

Add ears, eyes, nose, mouth, and other details

4

Erase overlapping lines, then add legs

5

Add more details by filling in ears and adding fur and a blanket

6

Finalize your lines with a marker or pen

HORSE

1

Sketch some basic shapes to create the head and mane of your horse

2

Add a circle for the body

3

Erase overlapping lines, then add snout

4

Erase overlapping lines, then add neck and detail to mane

5

Erase overlapping lines, then add eyes, forelock, and ears

6

Add ear detail, nostril, mouth, and back detail, then erase overlapping line

7

Erase overlapping lines, then add top of legs

8

Add bottom of legs and tail

9

Finalize your lines with a marker or pen

BARN

1

Sketch a few rectangles and lines

2

Add a roof

3

Add more details to your doors and windows

4

Add wood and grass texture

HAY BALE

1

Sketch some basic shapes

2

Add crossed lines

3

Add texture

FLOWERS

1

Draw curved lines

2

Add teardrop shapes for leaves

3

Add cloud shapes for flowers

PICKET FENCE

1

Draw 6 straight lines

2

Connect the lines horizontally and add triangle peaks

3

Add grass and wood detail

7

FOREST CREATURES

FOX · BEAR · SQUIRREL · HEDGEHOG

FOX

1

Sketch some basic shapes to create the head, body, and ears of your fox

2

Erase, then add triangle shapes for cheeks and a diamond shape for the snout

3

Erase overlapping lines, then add eyes, nose, fur, and front legs

4

Erase overlapping lines, then add hind legs and tail

5

Erase overlapping lines, then add more detail to the head, ears, body, and tail

6

Finalize your lines with a marker or pen

BEAR

1

Sketch some basic shapes to create the head and body of your bear

2

Erase overlapping lines, then add more shapes for ears, snout, and belly

3

Add eyes, nose, inner ears, and mouth

4

Erase overlapping lines, then add legs and arms

5

Erase overlapping lines, then add texture and detail

6

Finalize your lines with a marker or pen

SQUIRREL

1

Sketch some basic shapes to create the head and body of your squirrel

2

Erase overlapping lines, then connect head to body and add facial features

3

Add ears, teeth, and legs, then erase overlapping lines; add fur to back of head

4

Erase overlapping lines, then add arms and nut

5

Erase overlapping lines, then add feet

6

Add tail

7

Add more detail, like whiskers and fur

8

Finalize your lines with a marker or pen

HEDGEHOG

1

Sketch some basic shapes to create the head, ears, legs, and body of your hedgehog

2

Erase overlapping lines, then add hair, snout, and toes

3

Add eyes and nose

4

Add ear detail and arms

5

Erase overlapping lines, then add spiky texture using short, quick strokes

6

Finalize your lines with a marker or pen

OAK TREE

1

Draw a cloud shape

2

Draw straight lines to create trunk

3

Add trunk texture

4

Add leaves, grass, and other details

DEN

1

Draw a squiggle line and half oval shape to create a hill

2

Add grass and other details

BUSH

1

Draw a cloud shape

2

Draw a rectangle and line at the bottom

3

Add berries or leaf texture

ACORN

1

Draw an oval shape with a point at the top

2

Draw two curved lines that meet at the bottom

3

Add texture

8

SAFARI
ANIMALS

ELEPHANT · GIRAFFE

ELEPHANT

1

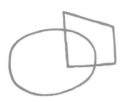

Sketch some basic shapes to create the head and body of your elephant

2

Erase overlapping lines, then draw two shapes to create ears

3

Erase overlapping lines, then add trunk, mouth, tail, and eyes

4

Erase overlapping lines, then add legs

5

Add more detail to the face, feet, and trunk

6

Finalize your lines with a marker or pen

GIRAFFE

1

Sketch some basic shapes to create the head and body of your giraffe

2

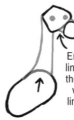

Erase overlapping lines, then connect the head and body with two curved lines, adding eyes

3

Erase overlapping lines, then add ears, horns, mouth, nostrils, and mane

4

Erase overlapping lines, then add top of legs

5

Add bottom of legs and tail

6

Add spots and hooves

7

Finalize your lines with a marker or pen

ACACIA TREE

1

Draw a cloud shape

2

Add a trunk

3

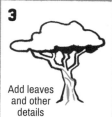

Add leaves and other details

WATERFALL

1

Draw lines to make a hill

2

Draw some half ovals to create mountains, rocks, and water

3

Add cloud shapes to create a tree and bushes; add a trunk and grass

4

Add texture and other details

9

REPTILES & AMPHIBIANS

SNAKE · FROG · LIZARD

SNAKE

1

Draw a wavy line and an oval to create the body and head of your snake

2

Erase overlapping lines, then draw another wavy line

3

Add mouth, eyes, spots, and belly lines

4

Finalize your lines with a marker or pen

FROG

1

Draw some basic shapes to create the head and body of your frog

2

Erase overlapping lines, then add straight lines to create legs

3

Add eyes, mouth, scalloped lines for feet, and details

4

Finalize your lines with a marker or pen

LIZARD

1

Draw some basic shapes to create the head and body of your lizard

2

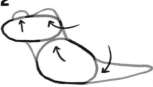

Erase overlapping lines, then connect the head to the body and draw top of head and a triangle for a tail

3

Add eyes, nostrils, and mouth

4

Erase overlapping lines, then add legs

5

Add details, like spots and belly lines

6

Finalize your lines with a marker or pen

TROPICAL PLANT

1

Draw some curved lines

2

Draw heart shapes at the ends to make leaves

3

Add dirt

TROPICAL PLANT WITH LOG

1

Draw some straight and curved lines to create a log

2

Add some more lines and an oval shape to create dirt and rocks

3

Draw some curved lines to create blades of grass

4

Add more detail

10
AQUATIC
ANIMALS

FISH · WHALE

FISH

1
Draw an oval and a circle

2
Erase, then add eye and fins

3
Add more detail, like scales and stripes

4
Finalize your lines with a marker or pen

1
Draw triangles and a circle

2
Erase, then add pupil, mouth, and fin

3
Add stripes and other details

4
Finalize your lines with a marker or pen

1
Draw a triangle

2
Erase, then add eye, mouth, and fins

3
Add more detail

4
Finalize your lines with a marker or pen

1
Draw some basic shapes

2
Erase overlapping lines, then add pupil, mouth, gill, and other details

3
Add more detail, like fin stripes

4
Finalize your lines with a marker or pen

WHALE

1

Sketch a teardrop shape to create the body of your whale

2

Erase overlapping lines, then add a mouth and fins

3

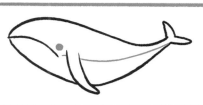

Add an eye and lines to show where the whale's belly begins

4

Add more details

5

Finalize your lines with a marker or a pen

SEAWEED

1

Draw a few circles and wavy lines

2

Draw a few more wavy lines to create seaweed

3

Add bubbles and more details

CORAL REEF

1

Draw some basic shapes using wavy lines

2

Add some more wavy lines to create a coral reef

3

Add bubbles and more details

AQUARIUM

1

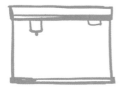

Draw some rectangles

2

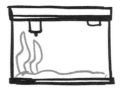

Add tank details

3

Decorate your tank and add bubbles

An imprint of Macmillan Publishing Group, LLC
120 Broadway, New York, NY 10271
OddDot.com

Library of Congress Cataloging-in-Publication Data is available.
ISBN 978-1-250-78368-4

Editors: Justin Krasner & Kate Avino
Designers: Christina Quintero & Tae Won Yu

Our books may be purchased in bulk for promotional, educational, or
business use. Please contact your local bookseller or the Macmillan
Corporate and Premium Sales Department at (800) 221-7945 ext. 5442
or by email at MacmillanSpecialMarkets@macmillan.com.

Show-How Guides is a trademark of Odd Dot.
Printed in China by Hung Hing Off-set Printing Co. Ltd., Heshan City,
Guangdong Province
First edition, 2021

10 9 8 7 6 5 4 3 2 1

Keith Zoo

is an artist and illustrator
living in Massachusetts. You
can find more of his work
at keithzoo.com and on
Instagram @keithzoo.